Understanding Samantha
A Sibling's Perspective of Autism

Dustin Daniels
Illustrations by **Jaehyun Lamia Bae**

Summary: David is the younger sibling to his sister Samantha, who has Autism. He is learning to understand her differences and decides to help her through a difficult time, by empathizing what her world is like. In the end, he has a better understanding of his sister's sensory issues.

ISBN-13: 978-1481994019

Understanding Samantha: A Sibling's Perspective of Autism

Text copyright © 2012 by Dustin Daniels

Illustrations copyright © 2012 by Jaehyun Lamia Bae

Self-published by Dustin Daniels

For more information about Dustin Daniels
please visit my website at www.UnderstandingSamantha.com

This book is dedicated to Haley and Michael, my children.

Understanding Samantha

A Sibling's Perspective of Autism

My name is David. This is my Dad and my older sister Samantha. She has autism.

My Dad explains that because of it, she thinks and acts differently. I don't always understand why she acts certain ways or says certain things. It seems like she's in her own world much the time.

Today is Wednesday, one of my favorite days of the week, because that means it's game night at our house. We're going to play a game that my sister learned at Social Club.

She goes there during the week to work on social skills. It's a special type of school where she learns how to get along with other kids.

Because of her autism, sometimes Samantha gets anxious and doesn't know how to use the right words to tell us that she needs a break.

When this happens she gets distracted by something else and it usually puts a stop to what we are doing.

It's Samantha's turn to go in the game, but her attention is somewhere else in the room. I can see that there is a butterfly flying near the window.

Insects are one of the things that she can get easily distracted by.

Samantha is squeaking in a high-pitched voice and yelling, "buggy, buggy, buggy!" My dad calls this 'stemming' and says that she does this to release some of her anxiety.

This is why I sometimes don't like to play games with my sister. We try not to play games that take a lot of time. When this happens, we all have to stop until she can focus again.

Usually the stemming will get louder and louder until my dad can calm her down. She will sometimes go into a tantrum and get angry before we figure out what she wants.

Samantha is more sensitive to her surroundings than most people.

I decide that tonight is going to be different. I try to think like Samantha, and what I could do to help her relax more. While my sister is running around the house, I go into her bedroom and look around.

I try to figure out how to make her environment more peaceful for her.

The first thing I notice is that the room is illuminated with the bright yellow rays of the afternoon sunlight coming in through the window.

I remember that Samantha is more sensitive to light than most people...

I pull the blinds on the window shut.

As I do, the colors in the room transform from a golden yellow, to a deep relaxing ocean blue.

With the light in the room more muted, I become more conscious of the common sounds around me. I can hear the whirring of the ceiling fan and the ticking of a clock's second hand on the wall.

Samantha is more sensitive to sound than most people...

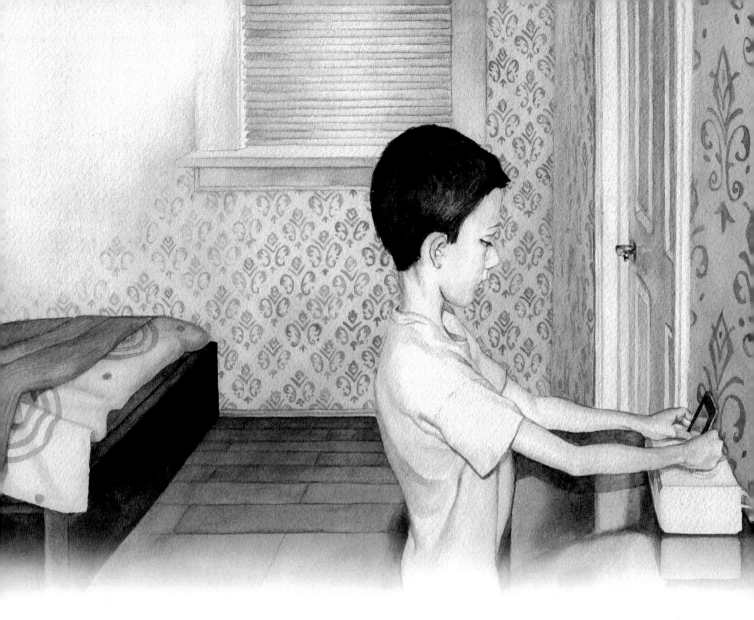

I find a song on her music player titled, "Ocean Waves" and put it in the stereo on Samantha's nightstand.

As it starts playing, I can hear the ocean waves begin to filter out the other noises in the room.

I pull out a yoga mat that is carefully tucked under her bed and roll it out across the floor.

The room seems more peaceful with the calm sounds of waves crashing on the beach.

I notice Samantha in the hallway approaching her room.

Samantha walks in and looks down at the floor. She isn't stemming any longer and sees me standing there.

I get a slight, but warm smile from her, then she lies down on the yoga mat on the floor.

She closes her eyes and I watch her whole body start to relax.

She begins to take deeper and deeper breaths.

Her stomach slowly rises and falls in sequence with the sound of the waves.

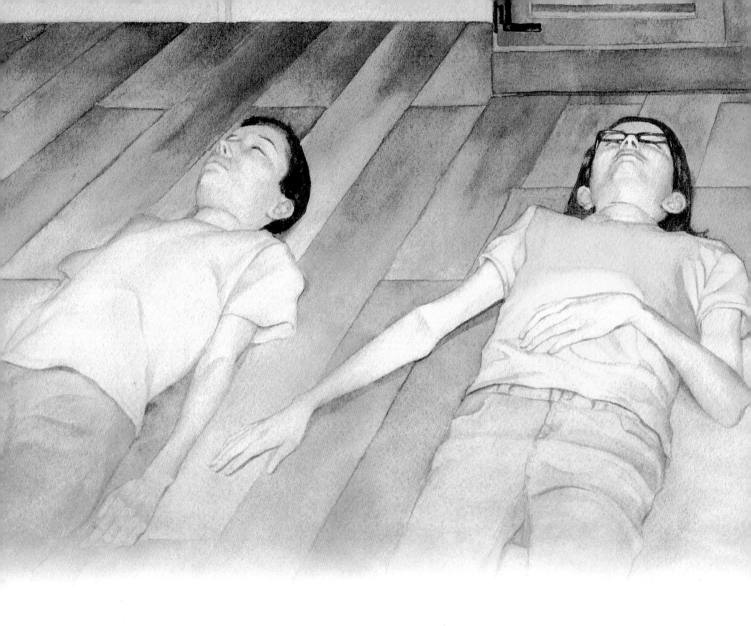

Samantha slowly opens her eyes and glances up at me. She pats on the floor next to her, inviting me to join.

I lay down next to her and close my eyes too. As I focus in on the sound of waves, I close off my other senses to everything around me.

I start taking deep breaths in tandem with my sister. As I listen to the soothing rhythm of crashing ocean waves, I am aware of myself feeling more relaxed.

I remember that Samantha is more sensitive to the way her body feels...

Sometimes I don't always understand why my sister acts the way that she does because of her differences...

I know it must be tough for her to have to adjust to our world.

Tonight, I'm glad I got to connect with Samantha in hers.

Made in the USA
Monee, IL
31 May 2022

97301658R00017